the little book of

CRYSTAL
MAGIC

First published in 2025 by OH
An Imprint of HEADLINE PUBLISHING GROUP LIMITED

1

Disclaimer:
This book is intended for general informational purposes only and should not be relied
upon as recommending or promoting any specific practice, diet or method of treatment.
It is not intended to diagnose, advise, treat or prevent any illness or condition and is not
a substitute for advice from a professional practitioner of the subject matter contained in
this book. You should not use the information in this book as a substitute for medication,
nutritional, diet, spiritual or other treatment that is prescribed by your practitioner.
Furthermore, the publisher is not affiliated with and does not sponsor or endorse any
uses of or beliefs about in any way referred in this book.

Cataloguing in Publication Data is available from the British Library

ISBN 978-1-03542-254-8

Compiled and written by: Katalin Németh
Editorial: Saneaah Muhammad
Designed and typeset in Joanna Sans Nova by: Stephen Cary
Project manager: Russell Porter
Illustrations: Freepik.com
Production: Rachel Burgess
Printed and bound in China

Headline's policy is to use papers that are natural,
renewable and recyclable products and made from wood
grown in well-managed forests and other controlled
sources. The logging and manufacturing processes are
expected to conform to the environmental regulations of
the country of origin.

HEADLINE PUBLISHING GROUP LIMITED
An Hachette UK Company
Carmelite House, 50 Victoria Embankment, London EC4Y 0DZ

The authorised representative in the EEA is Hachette Ireland, 8 Castlecourt Centre, Dublin
15, D15 XTP3, Ireland (email: info@hbgi.ie)

www.headline.co.uk   www.hachette.co.uk

the little book of
CRYSTAL
MAGIC

katalin németh

CONTENTS

INTRODUCTION

Please seek the advice of a professional if you suffer from any illnesses mentioned. Crystal healing is a complementary therapy that enhances but never replaces traditional medicine or professional therapy.

For centuries, crystals have captivated us with their beauty, mystery and powerful energies.

From ancient civilizations to modern-day healers, people have turned to these natural treasures to amplify intentions, manifest desires and connect with the unseen forces of the universe.

In this little book we dive into the fascinating world of stones, gems and minerals to discover how these earth-born wonders can be used for healing, protection, manifestation and personal transformation.

Whether you're new to crystal magic or have been working with these tools for years, this book will guide you through the foundational principles of harnessing their energy and magic.

You'll learn how to select, cleanse and charge your crystals, as well as how to align them with your intentions to enhance your spiritual practice.

From love and abundance to protection and balance, each crystal holds a unique vibration that can unlock doors to your highest potential.

Remember, if you use crystals for any form of healing, ensure that you consult with a medical professional and use the crystals alongside any previously prescribed medication.

CHAPTER

1

WHAT makes CRYSTALS MAGICAL?

UNIQUE VIBRATIONAL FREQUENCY

The power of crystals lies in their vibration. Each crystal has a specific molecular structure that gives it a unique vibrational frequency.

These vibrations interact with our energy fields (or aura), promoting healing, balance and alignment with different intentions.

CONNECTION TO THE EARTH

Crystals are born from the Earth's natural processes over thousands, or even millions, of years.

This deep connection to the planet gives them grounding energy, making them powerful tools for connecting us to nature and the larger universe.

SYMBOLIC PROPERTIES

Different types of crystals have long been associated with specific meanings and purposes. For example, rose quartz is known for love and compassion, while amethyst is often linked to spiritual protection and wisdom.

These associations enhance their magical appeal as tools for setting intentions and manifesting desires.

MAGICAL HEALING POWER

Crystals are believed to influence physical, emotional and spiritual well-being.

Through practices like crystal healing, crystals can help to clear blockages in the body's energy centres (chakras), remove negative energy and support personal growth and healing.

CHAPTER

2

WORKING
with
CRYSTALS

The crystals in this book are recommendations. Feel free to replace them with crystals that resonate better with you. It should feel right to you.

Although, in the forthcoming spells wands will be mentioned – the best crystal for a wand is clear quartz. It is great at conducting, storing and amplifying energy.

In these spells, you can say the
Wicca line:

"So it is and so mote it be"

or your own phrase, to seal the spell.

Many phrases will work, as long as they
are meaningful to you.

CHOOSING your CRYSTALS

There are hundreds of types of crystal that can be collected, all with different colours, shapes and sizes. It may seem daunting to start your collection, but as with all things in life, it's okay to begin one step, or one crystal, at a time.

Every crystal has a specific healing property; while many crystals have similar properties and effects, the feeling that each one provides to the individual is distinct from the others.

To choose your healing crystals, search for the different crystals that might provide the specific healing you are in need of. Consider its shape and size and how you will implement it in your everyday life – for example, wearing it as a necklace, keeping it as a feng shui piece or using it as a palm stone.

Once you have narrowed down the crystals that might work for you, you have a starting point for your collection! It is best to search for your crystals in spaces and stores where you are able to see and feel them – and where crystal experts are present to provide more details about each crystal.

If you feel overwhelmed by the selection of crystals, take a step back and allow yourself a moment to study each of them. There is often one crystal that you will feel drawn to – hold this crystal, close your eyes and allow yourself to sense its energy. If the crystal is meant for you, you're likely to feel a positive sensation, such as a soft buzzing, warmth, peace or joy.

If you aren't sensitive to subtle energies, choose the one you like the most based on its aesthetic. For example, to help with anxiety, you could choose a moonstone pendant.

It's okay if you aren't sensitive to subtle energies – you can still find the crystal that is right for you. A crystal can often stand out to an individual simply by the way it looks or the feeling you experience within yourself when the crystal is near.

It's always important to collect crystals from ethical sources and to be mindful of both the environment and those who mine the crystals.

CLEANSING your CRYSTAL

Before casting your spells, always cleanse your crystals. They might have residual energy attached to them from a former spell, or from invertedly infusing them with your vibrations throughout the day.

How frequently you need to cleanse your crystals will depend on how often you use them. If a crystal is in intensive daily use, such as a necklace worn continuously, it will likely need daily cleansing.

Use your intuition to determine how often your crystal should be cleansed, but your specimen gathering dust is usually a clear indication that it is time for a cleanse.

There are many ways to cleanse your crystals, and they all work equally well. The only thing to keep in mind is the structure of the crystal, because some might dissolve in water or become discoloured under the Sun.

Always consult your crystal seller if you are unsure, but the following methods of cleansing should work with any crystal, regardless of porousness.

SMUDGING

Smudging, or smoke cleansing, is one of the best ways to cleanse crystals.

Light a bunch of sage, bay leaves or even your favourite incense sticks, and cleanse your crystals by bathing them in the smoke and willing any residual energy to leave.

Open all the windows in the room, so any negative energy has a way to leave.

WATER

Most crystals are suitable to be cleansed with water. Take caution and check if water is safe for your crystal, ensuring that it does not damage the shine on the surface.

A safe way to cleanse a crystal is to carefully dab it with a wet cloth and then gently pat the crystal dry with a soft towel that you use specifically for cleansing. This method should work with virtually any crystal.

Other methods of cleansing include burying the crystal in the ground, submerging it in Moon water, using big clusters or wands of crystals, or by using the sound of instruments such as bells or singing bowls.

Some of these methods are not suitable for all crystals, so ensure that you research the effects before trying them.

CRYSTAL GRIDS

A crystal grid can be as simple as a cross of five crystals or as intricate as a sacred geometry pattern like the Sri Yantra or Flower of Life.

You can draw or paint the grid on paper or a ceremonial plate, print a pattern or buy one from a metaphysical shop. The key is to ensure it holds the crystals in place and is kept in a safe, undisturbed spot.

The page opposite displays an example of a simple grid.

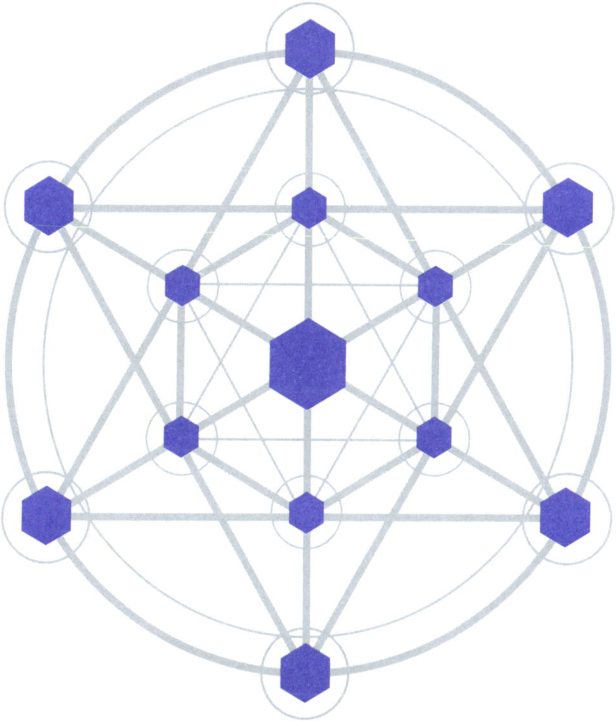

CHAKRAS

Chakra healing is beneficial for the whole body. If energy flows unhindered between the chakras, it can help to achieve good overall physical and mental health.

Crystal magic can help balance and open the body's chakras.

Clear quartz is the amplifier, so although it is not associated with a particular chakra, it will enhance the energy of the other crystals you use.

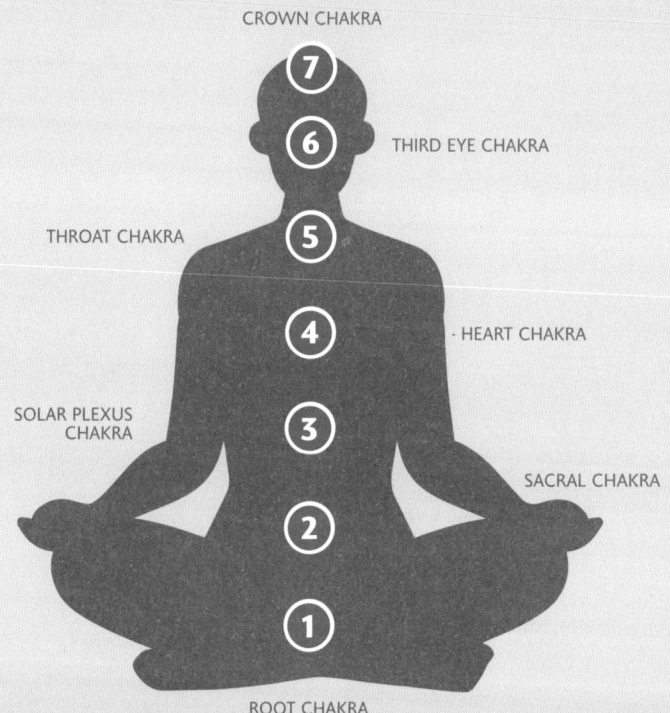

CROWN CHAKRA

7

THIRD EYE CHAKRA

6

THROAT CHAKRA

5

HEART CHAKRA

4

SOLAR PLEXUS
CHAKRA

3

SACRAL CHAKRA

2

1

ROOT CHAKRA

CLEAR your MIND

When casting any spell, your state of mind is what determines its success.

Before casting, ensure that you are present and focused. Remove distractions and still your mind with meditation or visualization.

A spell's success can rely on faith and belief in the spell itself, as well as the intention behind the spell.

Focus on the present, letting other worries fade to the background. Concentrate on the spell, mentally reviewing its steps and ensuring you have everything needed.

Start your spells only when you are free of doubts.

CHAPTER
3

PREPARING to WORK with CRYSTAL MAGIC

THE MOON

The Moon reflects light that it receives from the Sun. As it circles the Earth, rays of sunlight strike its surface and illuminate different portions of its face.

The Moon has a huge physiological effect on everything on Earth, especially anything that contains water. The human body is made of 60% water, so many believe that the phases of the Moon affect us as well.

To align yourself with the Universe, you can time your spells with the Moon's phases.

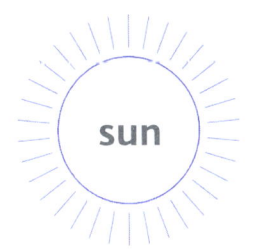

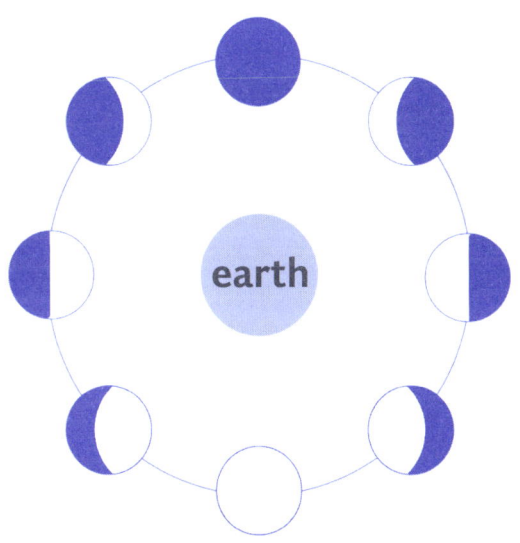

the WAXING MOON

The Waxing Moon is for growth, new beginnings and nurturing relationships.

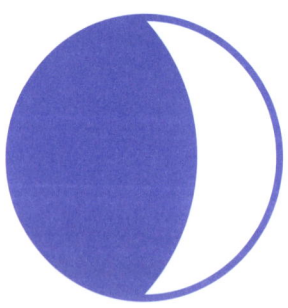

the FULL MOON

The Full Moon is for celebrating what you have, spiritual spells and charging your crystals.

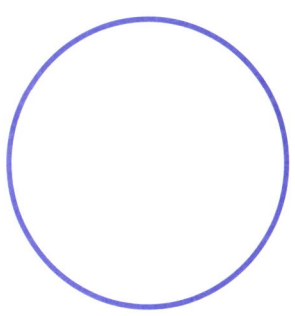

the WANING MOON

The Waning Moon is for letting things go, forgiveness, sharing and charity.

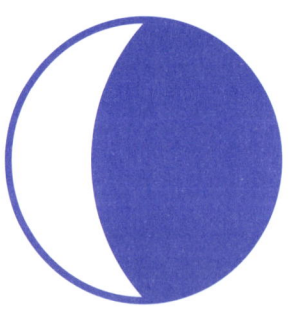

the NEW MOON

The New Moon is for letting go of what doesn't serve you, banishing spells and setting intentions.

the WHEEL of the YEAR

The Wheel of the Year represents the annual cycle of seasonal festivals or celebrations, marking the Earth's journey through the solar year.

It is typically divided into eight major festivals, often celebrated through rituals and ceremonies that align with the changing seasons and natural cycles.

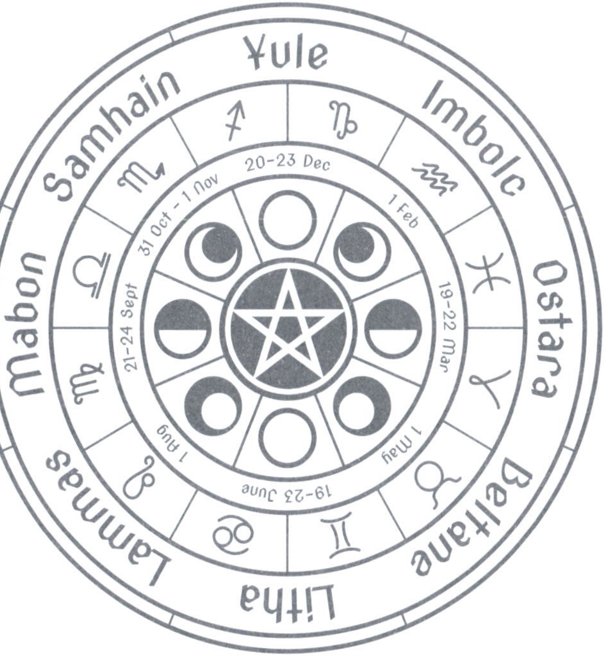

Yule

Samhain 31 Oct – 1 Nov

♐

♑ 20–23 Dec

Imbolc

♏

♒ 1 Feb

Mabon

♎ 21–24 Sept

Ostara

♓ 19–22 Mar

♍

♈

Lammas

♌ 1 Aug

Beltane

♉ 1 May

♋

♊ 19–23 June

Litha

Samhain: The Festival of the Ancestors and the start of the witches' new year.

Northern Hemisphere: 31 October
Southern Hemisphere: 30 April

Yule: The Festival of Returning Light falls on the Winter Solstice.

Northern Hemisphere: 20–23 December
Southern Hemisphere: 20–21 June

Imbolc: The Festival of New Life is the first season festival of the calendar year.

Northern Hemisphere: 1–2 February
Southern Hemisphere: 1 August

Ostara: The Festival of Fertility and Renewal falls on the Spring Equinox.

Northern Hemisphere: 19–21 March
Southern Hemisphere: 21–23 September

Beltane: The Festival of The Green Man welcomes in summer.

Northern Hemisphere: 1 May
Southern Hemisphere: 31 October–1 November

Litha: The Summer Solstice falls on the longest day of the year.

Northern Hemisphere: 20–21 June
Southern Hemisphere: 21–22 December

Lughnasadh: The Harvest Festival is a good time to practise your skills.

Northern Hemisphere: 1 August
Southern Hemisphere: 1 February

Mabon: The Autumn Equinox is the last festival of the Wiccan year.

Northern Hemisphere: 21–22 September
Southern Hemisphere: 21–22 March

the BOOK of SHADOWS

It is a good idea to keep a diary or a Book of Shadows to log the spells you perform.

Write down the date, intention, crystal and words you used, and follow up with the result achieved, externally and internally.

It is up to you how intricate you make your spells. Almost anything works, if you have practice in focusing your intention.

Ultimately, it is your own energy and intent that counts the most.

Don't forget, you decide how you do witchcraft. Learn the basics, learn about different paths and forge your own practice.

CRYSTAL RUNE ORACLE

Creating your own oracle set is the most efficient way of learning how to use the runes and to create a personalized, supercharged set of oracle stones.

Clear Quartz, Amethyst and Black Obsidian are all excellent stones for fortune telling. You can engrave the stones with the runes or use a permanent marker – just be sure you repaint the stones from time to time, as the letters will wear off.

AETTS

The Elder Futhark alphabet has 24 letters, and these are divided into three groups of eight letters, called Aetts.

You will need 26 tumble stone crystals that are roughly the same size and shape. You could choose one specific crystal to infuse the whole set with the same energy, or you could assign a specific crystal to each Aett (division of runes) or even to each rune.

Try to pick crystals that can easily be told apart by their colour.

Aett #1

- Associated with Freyja, the diety of love and war.

- Contains runes that relate to physical, earthly matters, like love, conflict, money and creation.

- Freyja's runes are Fehu, Uruz, Thurisaz, Ansuz, Riadho, Kenaz, Gebo and Wunjo.

- Crystals associated with Freyja are Amber, Carnelian, Citrine and Red Agate.

Aett #2

- Associated with Heimdall, the diety who guards Asgard from its enemies. He is the watchman who stands at the gates of Bifrost.

- Contains runes that relate to change and transformation.

- Heimdall's runes are Hagalaz, Nauthiz, Isa, Jera, Eihwaz, Pertho, Algiz and Sowelo.

- Crystals associated with Heimdall are Aventurine, Tiger's Eye, Cat's Eye and Hawk's Eye.

Aett #3

- Associated with Tyr, the diety of war and justice.

- Contains runes that relate to emotions, spirituality and our interaction with the world around us.

- Tyr's runes are Tiwaz, Berkana, Ehwaz, Mannaz, Laguz, Inguz, Dagaz and Othala.

- Crystals associated with Tyr are Bloodstone, Clear Quartz, Lapis Lazuli and Smokey Quartz.

After cleansing the crystals, hold them one by one, and while painting or engraving the runes into them, speak to them about the meaning of the runes.

For example, when painting Fehu onto the crystal you chose for it, tell the crystal that from now on, it means wealth.

You can add a Yes and a No crystal to the runes, to easily answer yes/no questions.

CHAPTER

4

CRYSTAL
MAGIC
for past life
REGRESSION

Past lives have a great effect on your present incarnation. Your talents, hopes, fears and hardships could be rooted in a previous life. You might have missed a life lesson, done something to incur bad karma or suffered greatly at the hands of another and couldn't let go of that pain.

Whatever the reason, trauma from past lives can make this life harder. Knowing what caused your current hardships can help to overcome them.

Past life experiences can manifest in many ways. An irrational fear of a certain thing, frequent headaches, the inability to learn a certain language – but there are positive examples as well.

An unusual talent for a certain thing; an unusually mature personality, especially in children; born-with psychic abilities – these all could indicate that a person has had many previous lives.

Remembering past lives is not a normal state of the mind. As humans, we are made to experience each life without remembering the last, to protect us in this current incarnation.

Therefore, only try to find out who you were if you are ready to deal with all that comes with it.

remember:

What matters is who you are now and how you make sure you learn your lessons in this life, so your soul can evolve. Strive to be the best person you can be, be mindful of others and help people where you can. You can't go wrong with that.

Past Life
REGRESSION
SPELL

For this spell you will need:

- a metatron's cube grid
- 3 **ancestralite** tumble stones
- 3 **turritella agate** tumble stones
- 3 **amethyst** tumble stones
- 3 **hematite** tumble stones
- **lapis lazuli** earrings or ring
- a **crystal wand**

Place the grid on your altar. Take the earrings or ring and place them in the middle of the grid, on the central circle.

Place the Hematite pieces on the circles that sit on the corners of the outer downward-pointing triangle.

Place the Ancestralite pieces on the circles that sit on the corners of the outer upward-pointing triangle.

You should have a crystal on every outer circle.

Place the Amethyst pieces on the circles that sit within the upward pointing triangle.

Place the Turritella Agate pieces on the circles that sit within the downward pointing triangle.

You should have a crystal on every inner circle.

Using your wand, point to the relevant crystal on your grid and say the following:

hematite:

"Thank you for grounding me in reality – the here and now. Protect me from getting lost, save me from drifting away."

ancestralite:

"Thank you for helping me overcome trauma and utilize strengths from my past lives without guilt."

amethyst:

"Thank you for opening my mind to what has been hidden from me. I use this opportunity to learn and grow."

turritella agate:

"Thank you for guiding my consciousness to see what is relevant for my growth."

lapis lazuli:

"Thank you for lending me the strength to step into the unknown and for opening my Third Eye to my past life that is most relevant to me right now. I infuse you with all these crystals' qualities, so you can enable me to see my past lives."

Put on the earrings (the left one first, and then the right) or place the ring on the ring finger of your left hand.

Lay down, make yourself comfortable and close your eyes. Ask yourself a question you want answered during this regression.

Direct your attention to your toes. Feel them go limp as tension leaves them through the earth. Move upwards, to your ankles, knees, hips, until your whole body is relaxed.

Visualize yourself stepping into an elevator. Push a button and know that it will take you to the most relevant past life, at the point where your question will be answered.

Feel the elevator move downwards and count down from ten. When you reach zero, you have arrived.

Visualize the elevator door opening
and stepping out into that life. What
do you see? Where are you? Is there
anyone else? What is the date? Who
are you? Try to see and think of as
many details as you can.

When you finish exploring that life,
step back into the elevator. Press the
button that will bring you back to the
top, feeling your consciousness return
to the waking state.

Slowly open your eyes, roll to your side and gently sit up. Drink some water, eat a piece of fruit, then take your journal, or Book of Shadows, and note down the experience.

Whether immediately or over time, the experience will unfold a clear meaning.

Take off the earrings or ring and thank them for their service. Place them back into the middle of the grid to finish the ritual.

Let a few days pass before completing another ritual, to allow your body and mind to process the experience.

When you feel ready, repeat the steps. With time, it will become easier to reach the memory. You might even have flashbacks in your normal state – though if they become too intenese, you can perform a protection and grounding spell.

MANIFESTATION
SPELL

Before performing this spell, search deep within yourself, and ask yourself the following questions:

Does this thing serve my higher self? Could I potentially hurt anyone by achieving my goal?

If your heart is clear, the spell will work.

For this spell you will need:

- 6 **clear quartz** tumble stones
- a white candle
- a seed of life grid (on a piece of paper)
- a **crystal wand**

On the night of a Full Moon, write your wish on the grid, with as much detail and clarity as possible, and place the paper on your altar.

Light the white candle, allow a few drops of wax to drop onto the middle of the paper and stand your candle on the grid.

Ensure it is safe and secure, all the while thinking about your wish.

Place the six Clear Quartz crystals around the candle, at the tip of each of the petals. Take your wand, and say these words:

Dearest Clear Quartz,
strong and pure,

Help me achieve what I long for,

Send this ripple off for me,

So it is and so mote it be.

Visualize the energy from your grid ripple out into the world, making the necessary adjustments to attain your wish.

Have no doubt in your mind that the spell worked. Let the candle burn down and leave the grid untouched overnight.

The next day, reclaim the crystals and fold the paper, keeping any wax left in it. Place the folded paper on your altar where it won't be disturbed.

Now continue with your day to claim the manifestation.

If your wish was
not meant to be and it
doesn't serve your
higher self, don't be
disheartened:
**something even
better awaits you**.

MAGICAL
CLEANSING
SOAP

Trauma and stress can leave you feeling unable to perform any magic at all. Self-doubt, burnout, low energy: they can all stop you from performing at your highest magical potential.

To remedy this, the following spell will help for you to perform magic.

For this spell you will need:

- soap – bar or liquid shower gel, as you prefer

- a **black tourmaline** tumble stone

- a **carnelian** tumble stone

- a **citrine** tumble stone

- a **unakite** tumble stone

- a **blue kyanite** tumble stone

- a **lapis lazuli** tumble stone

- a **selenite** tumble stone

- a **crystal wand**

The spell will programme the soap
to cleanse any chakras that may have
accumulated negative energy.

It will help to gently remove any
unwanted vibrations, so you can
function as your best magical self again.

Place the soap on your altar and surround it with your crystals, ensuring that each crystal is touching the soap.

Now programme each crystal to infuse the soap with its power by pointing to the relevant crystal with the wand and saying the following words:

black tourmaline

cleanses my Root Chakra.
After using this soap, my Root
Chakra will be balanced, and I will
be ready to create.

carnelian

cleanses my Sacral Chakra. After using this soap, my Sacral Chakra will be balanced, and I will be ready to create.

citrine

cleanses my Solar Plexus Chakra. After using this soap, my Solar Plexus Chakra will be balanced, and I will be ready to create.

unakite

*cleanses my Heart Chakra.
After using this soap, my Heart
Chakra will be balanced, and I will
be ready to create.*

blue kyanite

*cleanses my Throat Chakra.
After using this soap, my Throat
Chakra will be balanced, and I will
be ready to create.*

lapis lazuli

cleanses my Third Eye Chakra. After using this soap, my Third Eye Chakra will be balanced, and I will be ready to create.

selenite

cleanses my Crown Chakra. After using this soap, my Crown Chakra will be balanced, and I will be ready to create.

Leave the spell to work overnight.

Use the soap every day or only on special occasions, it is up to you.

You can reuse the crystals as many times as you like, after cleansing and recharging them.

CHAPTER
5

CRYSTAL
MAGIC
for
PROTECTION

Protective spells are present in every culture. From planting rosemary bushes in front of the house to ward off evil to wearing black crystals or the Nazar Boncuk as protective jewellery, these spells and practices have stood the test of time.

The following spells can be tailored to help protect you from specific earthly threats or even nightmares, involuntary astral projection or negative entities.

Tweak them to your needs or use them as they are.

General

PROTECTION
SPELL

Choose a black crystal – these crystals are powerful guardians.

For this spell, we are using **onyx**, but any other black crystal, such as **obsidian**, **jet** or **black tourmaline** will work.

This spell will help to protect you from generic negative influences throughout your day.

The stress from a traffic jam, an angry teacher or boss, a cranky toddler, a rude stranger; whatever life throws at you, this spell will protect your peace.

You might want to recharge the crystal daily, especially after a rough day.

To programme your crystal, hold it in both hands and feel its energy blend with yours.

Visualize its energy slowly embracing you, forming a protective layer around you.

While holding the stone in your hands,
say the following words:

Powerful Onyx, hear my plea,

From all bad vibes,
please guard me,

Help me keep my inner peace,

So it is, and so mote it be.

Thank the stone for its help and place it where it will guard you and stay near you – wear it as a necklace or keep it in your pocket or a bag that you keep close to you.

In times of need, remind yourself of its presence. It will help to absorb any negative energy that is directed at you.

General
Room

PROTECTION
SPELL

This spell will need four crystals, symbolizing the four corners of your room and the four main aspects of life that need protection: physical, mental and emotional, financial and psychic.

The spell will help to create a protective wall around your space and keep away any harm.

For this spell you will need:

- **carnelian** to protect your physical health

- **rose quartz** to protect your emotional and mental health

- **amethyst** to protect your psychic health

- **citrine** to protect your financial health

- a **crystal wand**

- a pouch that can hold all four crystals

Place your crystals on your altar, in the shape of a square.

Visualize your room, and as you programme each crystal with your wand, imagine the energy of those crystals enveloping that room.

Say each line three times:

Bright Carnelian,
bringer of fitness,

Keep my body free
from illness.

Gentle Rose Quartz,
do your part,

Bring compassion,
strengthen my heart.

Peaceful Amethyst,
defend this room,

Where harmful entities
cannot roam.

Abundant Citrine,
shining like gold,

Protect my wealth,
and add threefold.

Now collect the crystals and place them in the pouch.

Ideally, the pouch should be opaque and inconspicuous, to avoid others touching or looking at it.

Hang the pouch above or behind your door.

If that is not possible, hang it at the window from the curtain rail or keep it somewhere that represents people and energy passing through the room.

Recharge the crystals at least once a month.

HOUSE
PROTECTION
SPELL

While similar to the previous spell, this spell will help to protect the entire house, including those inside it, from any harmful energies, both spiritual and physical.

The four Tourmalines will help to reject negative intentions, while the Clear Quartz helps to purify anyone who enters the house.

For this spell you will need:

- 4 **black tourmaline** tumble stones

- 1 medium-to-large **clear quartz**

Place all the crystals onto your altar, forming a square with the Tourmalines and placing the Clear Quartz in the middle to represent your house.

If possible, position them in a way that corresponds with the cardinal directions.

Starting with the crystal in the east, touch them individually, moving clockwise and leaving the Quartz in the middle for last.

Repeat following words three times to each Tourmaline:

Black Tourmaline, dark as night,

Guard me from all kinds of plight,

Harmful intent can't enter,

It goes back to its sender.

Then to the clear Quartz, say three times:

Clear Quartz,
pure as an angel,

Guard this house from
any danger,

Purify all who enter here,

Only good vibes can
stay near.

If you have a garden, bury the Tourmalines outside in each corner of the space. Otherwise, place the Tourmalines in the outermost corners of the home.

Begin by facing east and bury or place
the stone that represented east on
your altar in that corner.

Then, moving clockwise, bury or place
all the Tourmalines, keeping the same
rule in mind: south to the south, west
to the west, north to the north.

Once finished, return inside, and pick
up your Clear Quartz. Place it near
the entrance, in a permanent position
where it won't be disturbed.

If you buried the crystals in your garden, there is no need cleanse or charge them because they are in their natural element, continuously being cleansed by the rain and charged by the Sun and the Moon.

You may bless them periodically, reminding them of their purpose.

If your Tourmalines are indoors, you may want to recharge them occasionally.

The only crystal you need to cleanse and recharge regularly is the Clear Quartz. This should be done at least once a month on a Full Moon night, or as often as you see necessary.

PROTECTION
from an
INDIVIDUAL
SPELL

This spell aims to reduce the negative energy from specific people.

It will not remove their free will – instead, it will help to distract them from the energy they feel towards you by reminding them of their own purpose.

For this spell you will need:

- a **carnelian** tumble stone

- a small bottle of **moon water**

- a garden hand spade (optional)

Cleanse and charge the Carnelian, then go out into nature. It could be a local park or a nearby forest, but avoid your own garden.

Ensure that you won't be disturbed and that you have permission to dig a small hole in the ground.

Sit on the ground and take a few deep breaths. Allow yourself to remember all the ways this individual has affected you.

Speak to your stone about how this makes you feel and express how this behaviour is also affecting the individual.

Task the stone to help this person find a positive, constructive outlet in their lives that will benefit them and ultimately distract them from affecting you.

Let the Universe decide what this outlet should be and believe in your heart that it will turn out for the best.

Dig a small hole in the ground and place the Carnelian into it, as if planting a seed. Cover it with earth and pour the Moon Water over it.

Visualize the Carnelian growing roots that reach and radiate light to this individual. You have planted this blessing in their life. Spend some time sitting with it, then say goodbye to the stone and leave.

This stone is best left alone permanently after the spell is complete.

PROTECTION
from GOSSIP and
LIES SPELL

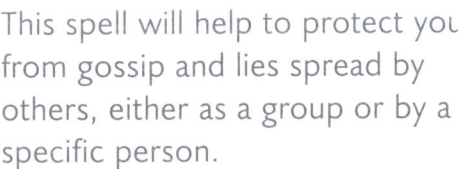

This spell will help to protect you from gossip and lies spread by others, either as a group or by a specific person.

The spell will not interfere with people's ability to speak, but it will aid in reducing the power of their words.

For this spell you will need:

- an **amazonite** tumble stone
- a glass jar
- pen and paper
- water
- black pepper, salt and vinegar
- aluminium foil

Write the name of the individual who is gossiping on your paper. Fold the paper in half and place it in the jar.

Fill the jar with water and mix in a teaspoon of black pepper and salt and a generous dash of vinegar.

Lock the jar and swirl it around, so that the ingredients are well mixed.

Take the Amazonite in your hands,
and programme it to bless this person
with integrity, honesty and clear
communication by saying these words:

*May (name of individual)
grow a backbone now,*

Karma shall find them, anyhow,

*Let them see reason and
not lie again,*

*Bless them with integrity,
truth deep within.*

Place the Amazonite on top of the jar and cover it with the aluminium foil, facing the shiny, reflective side of the foil inwards.

Concentrate on truth triumphing over lies.

When you are finished, place the jar into the freezer and leave it there until one month after the problem is resolved.

The crystal shouldn't need charging, but if you feel it is necessary, take it out of the freezer for a few hours, reprogramme the crystal and then re-wrap it with the foil and return it to where it was.

Once the problem has resolved and a month has passed, dispose of the jar. Let the ice melt completely, then take the jar far from your home and spill the water on the ground.

Dispose of the jar and the aluminium foil responsibly and keep the Amazonite. You may cleanse it and use it again later.

CHAPTER

6

CRYSTAL
MAGIC
for the MIND

Please seek the advice of
a professional if you
suffer from any illnesses
mentioned.

Crystal healing is a
complementary therapy that
enhances but never
replaces traditional medicine
or professional therapy.

Mental health is just as important as physical health, yet it is often neglected.

When mental health is poor, there is often a lack of energy or confidence needed for a complicated magic spell. This is why the spells below are more simple.

You could perform these spells for a loved one with their permission, if they are unable to do so themself.

Creating crystal elixirs is a wonderfully gentle way of making use of a crystal's power.

The crystal's vibration merges with the water's, creating a magical healing tonic that can carry all the benefits of the crystals that will work from within your body.

Tumble stones are great for this spell, but bigger specimens are preferred. Be mindful that some crystals dissolve in water, or release carcinogens.

The best practice is to keep the crystals next to, or over your jug or bottle or water, to infuse it with their power.

ANTI-DEPRESSION SPELL

For this spell, you will need:

- **citrine** and **lapis lazuli** tumble stones

- a bottle of water

Place the bottle of water on your altar or next to your bed. Place the crystals on either side of the bottle, ensuring that they are touching.

Say the following words:

*I infuse this water
with the liveliness of Citrine
and the optimism of
Lapis Lazuli.*

*It gives me the strength to
get out of depression.*

So mote it be.

Drink the entire bottle of water throughout the day and repeat the spell until you feel better.

ANTI-ANXIETY SPELL

For this spell, you will need:

- **moonstone** and **black tourmaline** tumble stones

- a bottle of water

Amber is another option if you need a stronger, more masculine energy to defeat anxiety. Place the bottle of water on your altar or next to your bed. Place the crystals on either side of the bottle, ensuring that they are touching.

Say the following words:

I infuse this water with the calmness of Moonstone, and the protective energy of Black Tourmaline.

It gives me the focus and confidence to defeat anxiety.

So mote it be.

Drink the entire bottle of water throughout the day and repeat the spell until you feel better.

INCREASE SELF-ESTEEM SPELL

For this spell, you will need:

- **black tourmaline** and **tiger's eye** tumble stones
- a bottle of water

Place the bottle of water on your altar or next to your bed. Place the crystals on either side of the bottle, ensuring that they are touching.

Say the following words:

I infuse this water with the fiery confidence of Tiger's Eye, and the clear-seeing energy of Black Tourmaline.

It reminds me that I am worthy of love and success, whatever that means to me.

So mote it be.

Drink the entire bottle of water throughout the day and repeat the spell until you feel better.

ANTI-TRAUMA SPELL

For this spell, you will need:

- **pink smithsonite** and **turritella agate** tumble stones
- a bottle of water

Place the bottle of water on your altar or next to your bed. Place the crystals on either side of the bottle, ensuring that they are touching.

Say the following words:

I infuse this water with the inner peace of Smithsonite, and the grounding and healing power of Turritella Agate.

It gives me peace and resolution to move on and heal.

So mote it be.

Drink the entire bottle of water throughout the day and repeat the spell until you feel better.

CHAPTER
7

CRYSTAL
MAGIC
for **LOVE** and
RELATIONSHIPS

Attracting the

RIGHT PARTNER SPELL

These spells will help you in every phase of a relationship – romantic or otherwise. As always, personalize them to supercharge their effect.

All relationship and love spells should be performed ethically.

Love magic is never about controlling or changing your partner but working on yourself and on your relationship to stay happily together, as long as you both want to.

This spell will request the Universe to bring the right person into your life. Begin this spell on the night of a New Moon and repeat it for 14 days, until the Full Moon.

For this spell you will need:

- a red pen and paper

- a **rose quartz** heart

- a red candle

Light your candle and place it on your altar. The candle should be large enough to burn for 14 minutes on 14 consecutive days.

You may use multiple candles, but ensure that you have enough for this duration.

If a candle runs out in the middle of your daily ritual, light a new one immediately.

Using your red pen, write down all the qualities of your perfect partner onto the paper. Make it as specific or as vague as you like. You could go into great detail about how they look, what they like, what they want from a relationship and how they should treat you, or you could say the following:

"I want to attract the person who is the best for me at this time, who supports my soul and my higher purpose and with whom we could heal together."

Set this list onto your altar and hold the Rose Quartz heart close to your chest.

Say the following three times:

Day by day, week by week,

Bring me partner closer to me.

Sit with the crystal for 14 minutes and contemplate the words on your paper.

Visualize the crystal enveloping you in a pink halo, acting as a beacon to your partner. Your radiance will attract them to you.

Once 14 minutes have passed, place the crystal onto the list and fold the paper around it. Extinguish the candle and go to sleep.

Repeat this ritual 13 more times.

On the last night, complete the ritual but amend the words you speak aloud:

Day by day, week by week,

You brought my partner closer to me,

They're now ready for us to meet,

So it is and so mote it be.

Wrap the crystal in the paper containing your list once again and place it under your pillow.

On this Full Moon night, you are likely to dream of your partner. You may not remember it in the morning, but when you meet them, you will recognize them in your heart.

The next morning, collect the packaged crystal from under your pillow and keep it on your person as you go about your day. Go out, meet people and be open to opportunities.

SELF-LOVE SPELL

It may sound cliché, but the most important thing to love is yourself. This spell will help to remind you of your worth, stick to your boundaries and walk away when you feel disrespected.

Begin this spell on the first day of the Waning Moon to release negative self-beliefs. The spell will complete on the next Full Moon, when you will be filled with positive self-confidence and self-love.

For this spell you will need:

- a seed of life grid
- 1 medium-to-large **rose quartz** piece
- 6 **aventurine** tumble stones
- 6 **obsidian** tumble stones

Place the Seed of Life grid on your altar in a stable position. It will hold your crystals for the duration of the spell, ensuring that it will remain undisturbed for the duration of the spell.

Hold the Rose Quartz against your heart. Feel its gentle, loving energy fill you up, like the embrace of a loved one.

Say the following words:

Thank you for teaching me self-compassion.

I am now able to accept myself as I am, and I love myself with my imperfections.

I forgive myself for the mistakes I made when I didn't know better.

I am ready to work on myself.

Place the crystal in the middle of the grid, where all the circles meet.

Now, hold the Aventurines close to your heart and feel your energies intermingle.

They should fill you with assertive peace, allowing you to focus on the love you feel for yourself.

Say the following words:

Thank you for teaching me assertiveness.

I am now able to give energy where it's needed and say no when necessary.

I am grounded in myself, and I don't need anyone's approval to feel worthy.

I am ready to consider my needs and rest when I must.

Starting with the northernmost flower, place the Aventurine crystals on the tips of the central flower's petals on the grid.

Hold the Obsidian crystals close to your heart. Feel their protective energy fill you with a sense of safety and determination.

Remind yourself that you will not cling to toxic relationships ever again, and that you are ready to let go.

Say the following words:

Thank you for teaching me how to draw my boundaries.

I am now able to enforce my boundaries, and I am strong enough to step away and leave if someone disrespects me

Starting from the east, place the crystals in the middle of the outer petals.

Leave the grid undisturbed until the next Full Moon and remind yourself of it often, remembering that it takes time for a new belief system to take root.

ENHANCING
SEXUAL DESIRE
SPELL

Perform this spell for yourself or
with a partner, ensuring that you
have consent, and performing it
together with your partner if they
are also magically inclined.

Further intimacy after this spell
may help to strengthen its power.

For this spell you will need:

- a **red jasper** tumble stone
- an **orange carnelian** tumble stone
- a red silk drawstring bag
- two red candles

If you are practising this spell with your partner, ensure that you have two of each crystal and two bags.

Light both candles and place them close together on your altar – ideally, they should touch.

If your candle holders don't allow it, tie the candles together with a red thread.

Hold the Red Jasper close to your pubic bone (this can be done over clothes).

Say the following words:

Thank you for reigniting my passion and inspiring me to be more sexually active and adventurous.

Place the Jasper in the bag.

Next, hold the Orange Carnelian close to your Solar Plexus chakra, between your navel and your ribs.

Say the following words:

Thank you for helping me feel desirable. I am ready to explore how to make our intimate time with my partner more exciting.

Place the Carnelian into the bag, alongside the Jasper.

Allow a few drops of wax from both the candles to fall onto the bag. The spell is complete. Keep the bag under your pillow or around your bed.

Allow the candles to burn down and have fun with your partner!

please note:

Do not complete this spell if you feel pressured. Instead, have an honest conversation with your partner about your wants and needs and about what they need from you.

CLOSURE
SPELL

Closure is necessary in many different areas of life and can often be the only thing holding us back. It is important for each of us to find our own closure.

For this spell you will need:

- a medium **selenite** tower

- a **blue lace agate** palm stone

- a **black obsidian** tumble stone

Hold the Selenite tower in both hands. Feel its cleansing power as it washes over you.

Allow yourself to remember the hurt that you have experienced and let yourself grieve. Cry if you are moved to, scream and shout if it makes you feel lighter. Let your emotions run free.

Once you feel more calm and the Selenite's energy feels soothing and centring, place it on your altar.

Hold the Blue Lace Agate palm stone between your hands in a prayer position.

Bring your hands close to your Third Eye Chakra, and say the following words:

Thank you for teaching me how to let resentment go.

Thank you for inspiring me to forgive myself for my own mistakes, too.

Place the Blue Lace Agate next to the Selenite on the altar.

Next, hold the Obsidian close to your Root Chakra, and say the following words:

Thank you for grounding me in reality. I will not let time tint my memories pink. I forgive, but I don't forget, and I learn from my mistakes.

If you are also seeking forgiveness and closure from your own actions, perform the same ritual, with the intention of forgiving yourself and becoming a better person.

OPEN
COMMUNICATION
SPELL

It isn't always easy to express your emotions and needs, especially if you are worried it might hurt someone else's feelings or ego.

This spell will help you express yourself in a clear yet soothing way and will help you let go of any anger or fear inside you that might prevent clear communication.

For this spell, you will need:

- a **blue lace agate** pendant for each participant (with a short chain or thread so that it sits close to the throat chakra).

You can perform this spell on your own, or with others if they are so inclined, to mutually strengthen communication.

As always, ask for consent if you perform this spell for someone else.

Hold your crystal to your throat and sing your favourite song, infusing the crystal with your voice and infusing your Throat Chakra with the crystal's energy.

While singing, focus your attention on how freely the sounds flow, and imagine the crystal retaining this memory.

When the song ends, say the following words:

Thank you for teaching me honest and clear communication.

I will leave destructive emotions out of expressing myself. I will not take others' communication as a personal attack.

I will strive to reach a mutually beneficial solution to any problem.

So mote it be.

Tie the string with the pendant on it on your neck and wear it continuously when you are awake.

Remove it when you sleep to recharge it, and when you bathe or shower, to avoid damaging the necklace.

CHAPTER

8

ENHANCING PSYCHIC ABILITIES

If you are familiar with witchcraft, it's useful to work with spells that can enhance your current abilities.

Crystals are the perfect way to further your magic, allowing you to merge your own energy with the energy of crystals.

This spell will help to unlock or further enhance any psychic ability, while allowing you to stay grounded.

Grounding is important in order to reduce becoming overwhelmed in the psychic realm.

For this spell you will need:

- a **selenite** wand
- a **moss agate** palm stone

Sit in front of your altar, holding the Selenite wand in your left hand and the Moss Agate palm stone in your right.

Face the Moss Agate in the direction of the earth, holding it close to the ground, and say the following words:

I am connected and protected by Mother Earth.

She keeps me grounded, and safe from negative influences.

Now point the Selenite wand towards
the sky. Lift it as high as you can, and
say the following words:

*I am connected to the sky,
protected by my spirit guides.*

*They teach me the art of
(the skill you want to learn)
and bless me with their power.*

Visualize the Moss Agate growing roots into the ground and anchoring you into this realm. Feel the magma in the Earth's core fill you up with warm, grounded energy. Allow it to enter through your Root Chakra and rise to your Heart Chakra.

Visualize the Selenite channelling spiritual energy from above. It enters through your Crown Chakra and descends all the way to your Heart Chakra, where it meets the Earth's energy flow.

Visualize these energies merging inside your body. You are now of both worlds, as above, so below.

Feel this wonderful sensation envelope your whole being, then feel it slowly recede to concentrate in your Heart Chakra.

You may lower your hand now and finish the ritual by thanking Mother Earth and your spirit guides.

From now on, whenever you practice your craft, this celestial energy will radiate out from your Heart Chakra into your Root Chakra to ground and protect you, and into your Third Eye or Crown Chakra, to connect you to the spirit world.

*I wish you joy
and success in your practice!*

Blessed be!